Start Writing About People and Places

Penny King
Ruth Thomson

Belitha Press

First published in the UK in 2000 by

 Belitha Press Ltd
London House, Great Eastern Wharf,
Parkgate Road, London SW11 4NQ

ISBN 1 84138 226 4 (hardback)
ISBN 1 84138 228 0 (paperback)

British Library in Publication Data for this book
is available from the British Library.

Series editors: Mary-Jane Wilkins, Stephanie Turnbull
Designers: Rachel Hamdi, Holly Mann, Angie Allison
Illustrators: Beccy Blake, Kevin Maddison, Melanie Mansfield, Lisa Smith
Educational consultants: Pie Corbett, Poet and Consultant
   to the National Literacy Strategy; Sarah Mullen, Literacy Consultant

Printed in China

Contents

How to use this book

Do you know how to write a convincing advert, a thrilling recount or clear instructions?

This book will show you lots of different kinds of non-fiction writing.

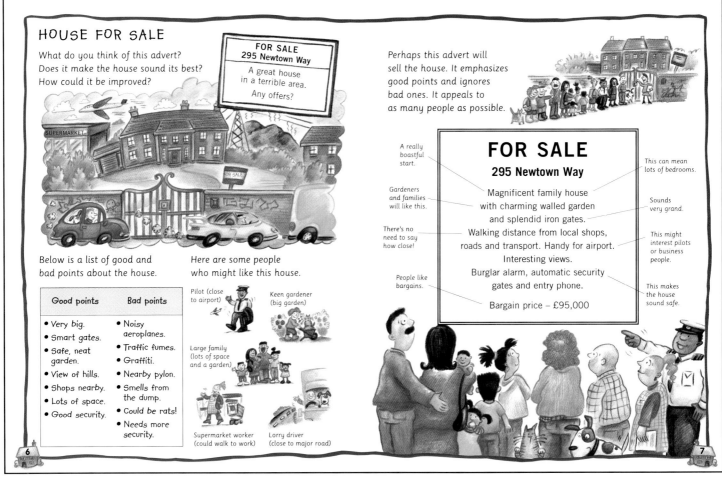

There are two double pages for each style of writing. The first one (see the example above) shows you how to plan your writing and gives you a model of a finished letter, advert, recount or chart.

Sometimes there are labels to help you, or a table like the one on the right.

Good points	Bad points
• Very big.	• Noisy aeroplanes.
• Smart gates.	• Traffic fumes.
• Safe, neat garden.	• Graffiti.
• View of hills.	• Nearby pylon.
• Shops nearby.	• Smells from the dump.
• Lots of space.	• Could be rats!
• Good security.	• Needs more security.

The second double page (see the example below) gives you step-by-step instructions to create your own piece of writing.

Read the instructions carefully before you start writing.

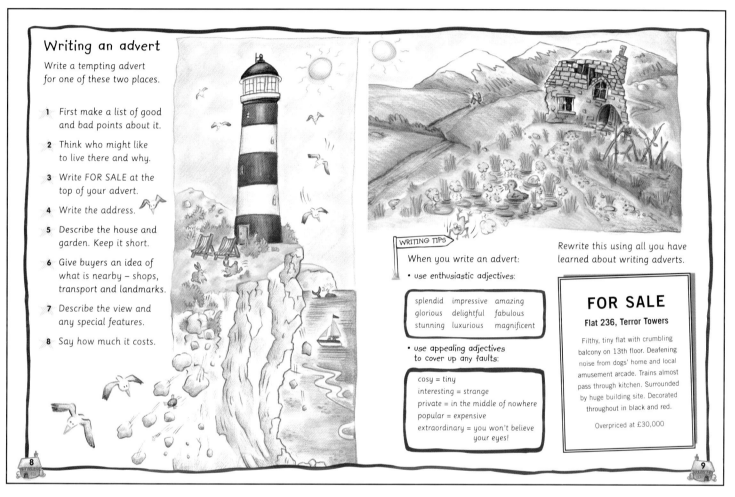

Writing an advert

Write a tempting advert for one of these two places.

1 First make a list of good and bad points about it.
2 Think who might like to live there and why.
3 Write FOR SALE at the top of your advert.
4 Write the address.
5 Describe the house and garden. Keep it short.
6 Give buyers an idea of what is nearby – shops, transport and landmarks.
7 Describe the view and any special features.
8 Say how much it costs.

WRITING TIPS

When you write an advert:

• use enthusiastic adjectives:

splendid   impressive   amazing
glorious   delightful   fabulous
stunning   luxurious   magnificent

• use appealing adjectives to cover up any faults:

cosy = tiny
interesting = strange
private = in the middle of nowhere
popular = expensive
extraordinary = you won't believe your eyes!

Rewrite this using all you have learned about writing adverts.

FOR SALE

Flat 236, Terror Towers

Filthy, tiny flat with crumbling balcony on 13th floor. Deafening noise from dogs' home and local amusement arcade. Trains almost pass through kitchen. Surrounded by huge building site. Decorated throughout in black and red.

Overpriced at £30,000

8

9

The writing tips explain the particular rules for each style of writing.

The pictures are full of extra ideas to make your writing come alive.

Sometimes there is a box of useful verbs or adjectives.

Enthusiastic adjectives:

splendid   impressive   amazing
glorious   delightful   fabulous
stunning   luxurious   magnificent

You can either use these suggestions or think of other suitable words.

HOUSE FOR SALE

What do you think of this advert?
Does it make the house sound its best?
How could it be improved?

FOR SALE
295 Newtown Way

A great house
in a terrible area.

Any offers?

Below is a list of good and
bad points about the house.

Good points	Bad points
• Very big.	• Noisy aeroplanes.
• Smart gates.	• Traffic fumes.
• Safe, neat garden.	• Graffiti.
• View of hills.	• Nearby pylon.
• Shops nearby.	• Smells from the dump.
• Lots of space.	• Could be rats!
• Good security.	• Needs more security.

Here are some people
who might like this house.

Pilot (close to airport)

Keen gardener (big garden)

Large family (lots of space and a garden)

Supermarket worker (could walk to work)

Lorry driver (close to major road)

Perhaps this advert will sell the house. It emphasizes good points and ignores bad ones. It appeals to as many people as possible.

A really boastful start.

This can mean lots of bedrooms.

Gardeners and families will like this.

Sounds very grand.

There's no need to say how close!

This might interest pilots or business people.

People like bargains.

This makes the house sound safe.

FOR SALE
295 Newtown Way

Magnificent family house
with charming walled garden
and splendid iron gates.
Walking distance from local shops,
roads and transport. Handy for airport.
Interesting views.
Burglar alarm, automatic security
gates and entry phone.

Bargain price – £95,000

Writing an advert

Write a tempting advert for one of these two places.

1   First make a list of good and bad points about it.

2   Think who might like to live there and why.

3   Write FOR SALE at the top of your advert.

4   Write the address.

5   Describe the house and garden. Keep it short.

6   Give buyers an idea of what is nearby – shops, transport and landmarks.

7   Describe the view and any special features.

8   Say how much it costs.

WRITING TIPS

When you write an advert:

- use enthusiastic adjectives:

> splendid   impressive   amazing
>
> glorious   delightful   fabulous
>
> stunning   luxurious   magnificent

- use appealing adjectives to cover up any faults:

> cosy = tiny
>
> interesting = strange
>
> private = in the middle of nowhere
>
> popular = expensive
>
> extraordinary = you won't believe your eyes!

Rewrite this using all you have learned about writing adverts.

FOR SALE

Flat 236, Terror Towers

Filthy, tiny flat with crumbling balcony on 13th floor. Deafening noise from dogs' home and local amusement arcade. Trains almost pass through kitchen. Surrounded by huge building site. Decorated throughout in black and red.

Overpriced at £30,000

PACKING UP

Mrs Jones is moving house. She has many precious possessions to pack. This calls for some clear instructions.

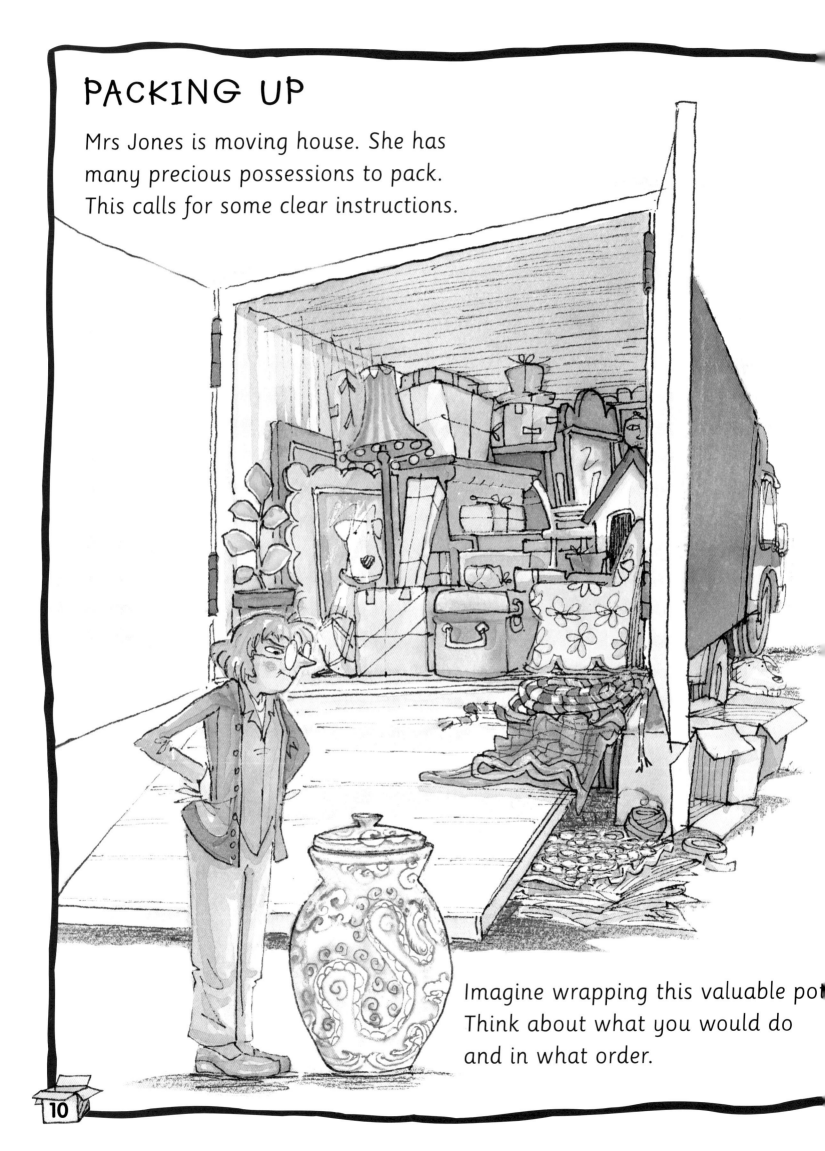

Imagine wrapping this valuable pot. Think about what you would do and in what order.

Here is one way to pack the pot safely.
You may have thought of a different way.
It doesn't matter as long as the pot is safe.

How to pack a pot

You will need:

- newspaper
- bubble wrap
- strong tape
- strong cardboard box
- polystyrene chips
- marker pen

What you do:

1 Remove the lid and make sure the pot is empty.

2 Stuff the pot with screwed-up newspaper.

3 Wrap the pot first with newspaper, then with bubble wrap.

4 Use strong tape to keep the wrapping in place.

5 Wrap the lid in newspaper and tape it to the top
   of the pot.

6 Screw up some newspaper and put a layer
   in the cardboard box.

7 Put the pot carefully in the box.

8 Fill the box with polystyrene chips and bubble wrap.

9 Close the box with strong tape.

10 Label the box **FRAGILE**.

Writing instructions

Write clear instructions for
packing one of these items.

A huge glass tank full of fierce fish

Lots of frozen food

1 First think how
you would wrap
the object.

2 Write the title:
How to pack a...

3 Write the heading:
You will need

4 List the materials you need.
Write them in the order
that you will use them.

5 Write the heading:
What you do

6 Write exactly what to do,
step by step.

A set of delicate china

A fancy glass chandelier

WRITING TIPS

When you write instructions:

- write in the present tense.
- only describe one activity at a time.
- number each instruction.
- begin each instruction with a verb.
- start each instruction on a new line.

Use bossy verbs (imperatives) to explain exactly what to do.

place	use	protect	roll
label	fill	wrap	unscrew
stick	take	cover	remove
stuff	pack	empty	screw

POINTS OF VIEW

What do you think about doing homework? Do your parents think the same? Does your teacher agree?

What do your friends think? The best way to find out everyone's opinion about homework is to ask them.

I'm tired after school so I can't concentrate on homework.

Me

Homework keeps you out of mischief!

Granny

I try to help you but I just muddle you – I don't know how things are taught at your school.

Mum

Doing homework helps you learn to organize yourself and remember what to bring home.

Dad

When you have homework you don't have time to play with me.

Little brother

Teacher

Best friend

You can put people's opinions on a 'For' and 'Against' chart like this.

...e the
...ment
...e top.

...e this
...e top
...e left-
...column.

...t each
...reason
...a
...et point.

...with
...mment
...ut what
...think
why.

Children should do homework.	
For	Against
• Children practise what they learn at school. • Children learn more. • Children learn how to organize themselves. • Children are kept busy. • Children are more confident because they have learned things well.	• Children are very tired and can't do their best. • Parents may muddle children by explaining things wrongly. • Children don't have time for playing or their hobbies.
I think that children should do homework because it helps them learn.	

Write this at the top of the right-hand column.

For and against

Choose one of the statements on these pages. Think of reasons for and against it. The pictures give you some ideas.

1 First do some research. You might:
   • interview people you know.
   • write to people.
   • make a questionnaire.

2 Next make a chart. Put the statement at the top. Divide the page in half. Write 'For' in one column and 'Against' in the other.

3 Write as many reasons as you can in each column.

4 End with a conclusion saying what you think and why.

All children should be given pocket money.

Children should play sport every day.

WRITING TIPS

When you write your chart:

- start each opinion with a *bullet* point.
- when you write an opinion, try to think of the opposite view too.
- give a reason for your final decision: 'I think that... because...'

ALL ABOUT ANIMALS

Reports are factual. They explain the way things are. This information about penguins is from an animal handbook.

BIRDS Emperor Penguin

HABITAT

Emperor Penguins live in seas around Antarctica, in large groups called flocks.

APPEARANCE

The Emperor Penguin is the largest of all penguins.
Height: 1.15m
Weight: 30 kg

Small bill

Oily, waterproof feathers

Thick blubber keeps penguin warm

Wings used for swimming not flying

Small feet

Tail steers when bird is swimming

BREEDING

In the autumn, male and female penguins travel 100 km south to a nesting site. There, they meet a life-long mate. Three weeks later, the female lays one egg. She returns north to feed, leaving the male to care for the egg.

The male keeps the egg warm on his feet under a flap of skin. He does this for two months. He eats nothing and huddles together with other males to keep warm. When the egg hatches, the female returns to feed the chick. The male can feed at last.

FEEDING

Penguins are fast swimmers (up to 30 km per hour). They catch fish, squid and krill in their beaks which they eat under the water.

This report is based on the information and pictures found in the handbook.

Emperor Penguins

t look

Emperor penguins have black heads, wings and feet and white tummies. Their necks are bright yellow. They are the biggest of all the penguins.

re live

They live in Antarctica, which is a very cold place. They have waterproof feathers to keep dry and fat to keep warm.

Penguins have wings but they cannot fly, though they swim fast. They use their wings like flippers and steer with their tails. They catch their food while they are swimming.

What they do

Wings push along

Tail steers

Krill

Squid

What they eat

Their babies

In the autumn, penguins travel to nesting sites. The female penguin lays one white egg. The male puts it on top of his feet to keep it warm. The female goes away to eat. The male penguins stand close together to keep warm. They do not eat for two months. The female returns when the egg hatches and then the male can eat. Baby penguins are called chicks.

egg

egg cracks

chick

iter's own mments

I saw some chicks at the zoo. They had soft, fluffy, grey feathers instead of black and white ones. The mother was feeding them with fish straight from her mouth into theirs. Most people love penguins and we need to protect them.

A good ending

Writing a report

Write a report about giant pandas
or African elephants.

MAMMALS Giant Panda

HABITAT

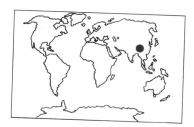

Pandas live alone in the
cold, high bamboo forests
in the mountains of China.

BREEDING

Female pandas produce
one or two babies (cubs)
every two or three years.
Cubs weigh only about
100g and have no fur.
Cubs need a lot
of care and usually
only one survives.

FEEDING

Pandas live mostly on
bamboo shoots and roots.
Sometimes they eat small
animals, birds and fish.
Adult pandas eat up to
38 kg of bamboo each day.

APPEARANCE

Height: 1.7m
Weight: Up to 150 kg

Eyes have good
night vision

Powerful jaws

Thick fur

Hairy feet
for walking on
snow and ice

Large paws
for grabbing
shoots
and roots

Sharp claws

---

1 First read the information.
Look up any words you do not
understand in a dictionary.

2 Make a list of the following
questions and jot down the
answers as you find them.

- What does the animal look like?
- Where does it live?
- What does it eat?
- What do you know about
  its babies?

MAMMALS African Elephant

HABITAT

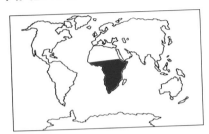

Elephants live in large groups called herds on the grassy plains of Africa.

BREEDING

Females (cows) give birth to one baby (calf) every four or five years. The calves weigh 90 kg and are 1 metre tall. They drink their mother's milk until they are six years old.

FEEDING

Elephants spend up to 18 hours a day grazing on grasses, leaves, roots, tree bark and fruit. An adult can eat up to 230 kg of food and drink 200 litres of water every day.

APPEARANCE

Height: 3.7m
Weight: Up to 7 tonnes

Thick skin

Large ears flap to cool elephant

Tail swishes flies away

Long trunk for smelling, sucking up water and picking up things

Tusks for digging and fighting

3 The neat copy. Write the title.

4 Write your report using the answers to your questions.

5 Add facts of your own. Look in other books to make sure they are correct.

WRITING TIPS

When you write a report:

• write in the present tense.

• start a new paragraph for every answer.

• end with a short conclusion.

A DREAM JOB

Imagine you have stepped back in time. You see this advert. What sort of letter would you write to persuade Captain Scott to take you with him?

Ed Venture made a list of his skills and talents.

WANTED!
Exceptional people
for the
adventure of a lifetime.
Expedition on foot
to
The South Pole

Apply in writing to:
Captain Robert Falcon Scott

Determined and brave

Excellent cook

Strong swimmer

Fit and healthy

Champion skier

Keen camper

Animal expert

Experienced fisherman

Skilled navigator

I hope he chooses me!

Ed Venture used his list to write a persuasive letter to Captain Scott.

He included as many reasons as possible to show why he was the best person for the job.

Address in the top right-hand corner

...gins with
...ar...'

...s things
...an do

...uasive
...uage

...ds with
...s

...ns his
...ne

Hill Farm
Kelso
Scotland
25th January 1909

Date under address

Dear Captain Scott,

I see from your advert that you are looking for exceptional people to travel with you to the South Pole.

I am 24 years old and very fit and healthy. I am an experienced fisherman and love being at sea. I am a very strong swimmer. While on the night watch I taught myself to navigate, using the stars. I am also an excellent cook.

I am sure it would be useful to have someone on your expedition who can look after animals. I am used to caring for animals and know cures for many common illnesses. I therefore think I would be a great help to you.

I have always dreamed of exploring unknown places, especially snowy ones, as I love to camp and ski.

Yours sincerely,

Ed Venture

This Ed Venture sounds just right for the job!